WITCHES FOUR

WITCHES FOUR

MARC ^TOLON BROWN

PARENTS MAGAZINE PRESS

New York

8007881

Copyright © 1980 by Marc Brown.

Printed in the United States of America.
10 9 8 7 6 5 4 3 2 1

Library of Congress Cataloging in Publication Data
Brown, Marc Tolon.   Witches four.
SUMMARY: Four witches discover their lost magic hats
have been found by four homeless cats and turned into houses.
[1. Witches—Fiction.   2. Stories in rhyme]   I. Title
PZ8.3.B8147Wi   [E]   79–5263
ISBN 0–8193–1013–1   ISBN 0–8193–1014–X lib. bdg.

FOR

• FOUR GOOD WITCHES •

BONNIE

COLLEEN

KIMBERLY

AND WEE KATHARINE

One witch,

two witches,

three witches,

four.

Not one less, not one more.
Everyone calls them WITCHES FOUR.

They each wear spectacles on their nose.
They dance together on forty toes.

They brush their teeth with

They eat bat-wing sandwiches.
They like the taste!

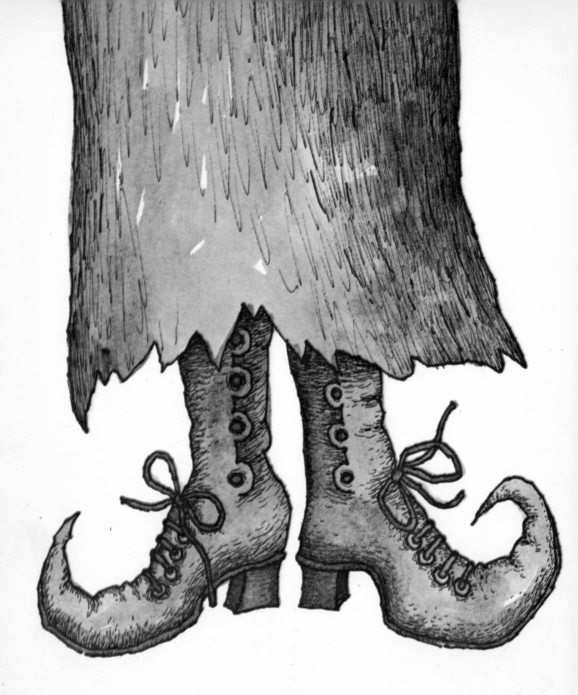

Witch boots on,
tied-up laces.

Frog-eye soap
to wash their faces.

Witches . . .
one,
two,
three,
four . . .
dressed for spooking
and out the door.

Witches on brooms.
Watch them zoom
over trains,
under planes.

TUCKER R.R.

They fly upside down
and lose their hats.

Four magic hats
fall down to the ground.

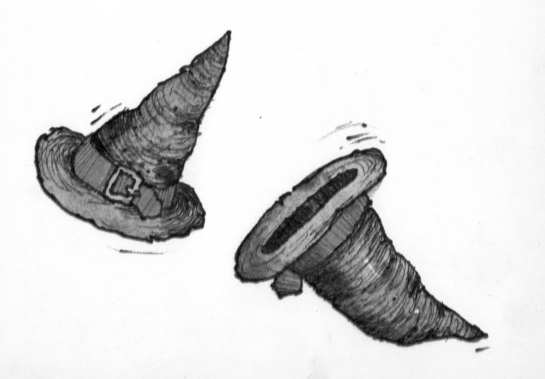

Four magic hats.

Four homeless cats.

"It's raining houses!"
said the cats. "How nice."
They moved right in
and dined on mice.

"Our hats are gone!
What shall we do?

No time to stop
for octopus stew."

One looked up.

One looked down.

One looked in the country.

One looked in the town.

Then by the tracks
they spied those cats
standing by the magic hats.
"We want our hats,
you silly cats!"

"Finders keepers,"
said the cats.
"These are our houses,
not your hats."

"We'll tell you to scram
just once more.
Then it's curtains!"
said WITCHES FOUR.

"No way," said the cats.
"Not a chance!"
They formed a circle
and started to dance.

"Fa, la, la," the four cats sang.
Then they heard the first big
CLANG!

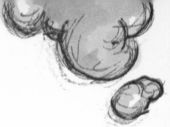

There were clouds of smoke
then KERBOOMS!

Four happy witches were off
on their brooms.

Four happy witches
with four magic hats.
And if you look very close,
you can find those cats!

About the Author

MARC BROWN gets many of his ideas for writing and drawing while he's traveling. He often can be found riding on trains, planes, or buses — to visit schools, see his publishers, or speak at conferences around the country.

At home in an old house near the sea in Hingham, Massachusetts, he develops his ideas into the words and pictures that will finally appear in his books. And all along the way, he shares them with children as often as he can, including his own two young sons.

Mr. Brown is making his second appearance on the Parents list. The first was as illustrator for Judy Delton's story *Rabbit's New Rug*.